365 First Words for LITTLE KIDS!

Dr. Meredith L. Rowe

Monika Forsberg

MAGIC CAT PUBLISHING

NEW YORK

Let's Get Talking

Toddlers are capable of learning a new word every day!

This bright, bold book is designed to provide a year's worth of words to grow your child's early vocabulary and will help fulfil their thirst for discovering the world around them.

We know that little ones are more likely to learn words when adults talk about the things children are interested in or focused on. The illustrations in this book will captivate a child's attention and provide opportunities for caregivers to label the objects or actions in the scenes. This book provides an easy and fun way to introduce new nouns and verbs into everyday vocabulary.

Meredith L. Rowe
Saul Zaentz Professor of Early Learning and Development
Harvard University, Graduate School of Education

Colors

Red

Yellow

Orange

One

Two

Three

Four

Five

Seven

Eight

Six

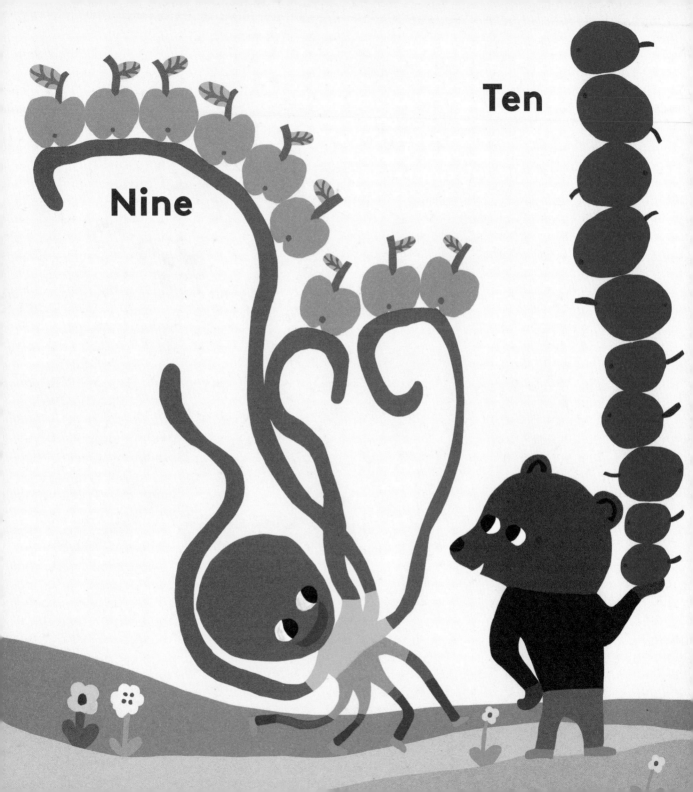

Nine

Ten

Diamond

Rectangle

Cross

Triangle

Grandpa

Grandma

Pet

Dad

Mom

Sister

Brother

Smell

Hear

See

Balance

Touch

Taste

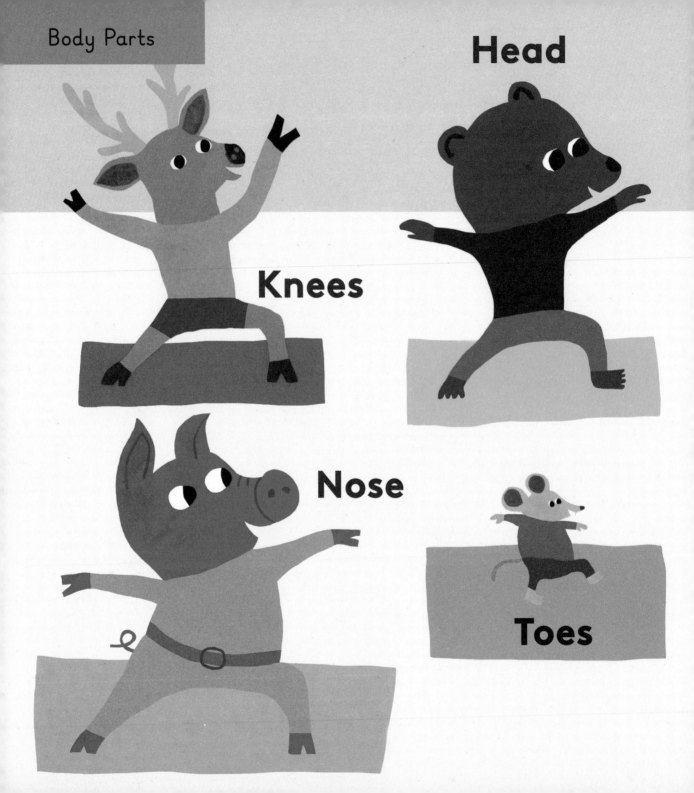

Body Parts

Head

Knees

Nose

Toes

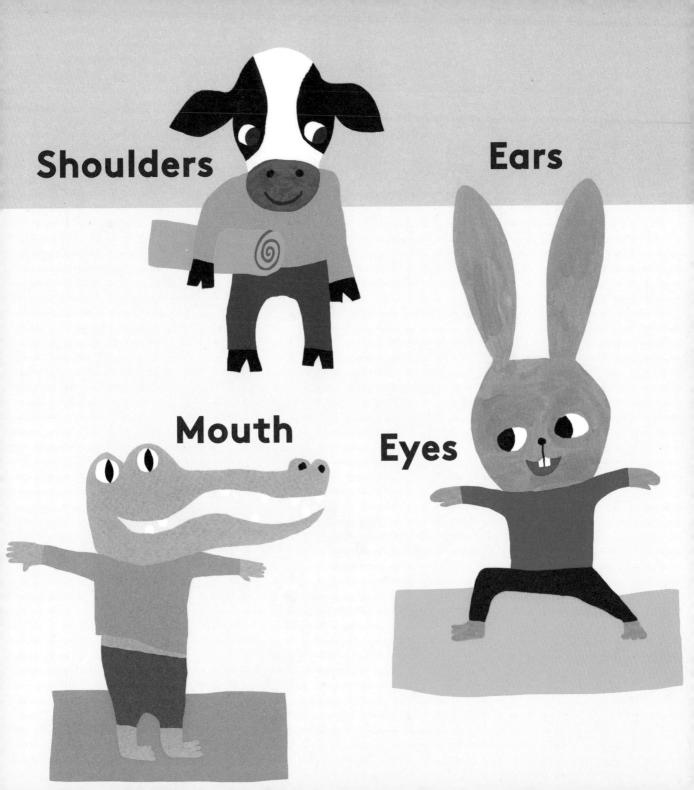

Shoulders

Ears

Mouth

Eyes

Clothes

Hat

Shorts

Top

Dress

Shoes

Socks

Diaper

Things That Go

Bus

Boat

Train

Car

Rocket

Bicycle

Tricycle

Watch

Wheelchair

Coat

Glasses

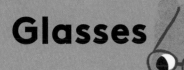

Mittens

Scarf

Umbrella

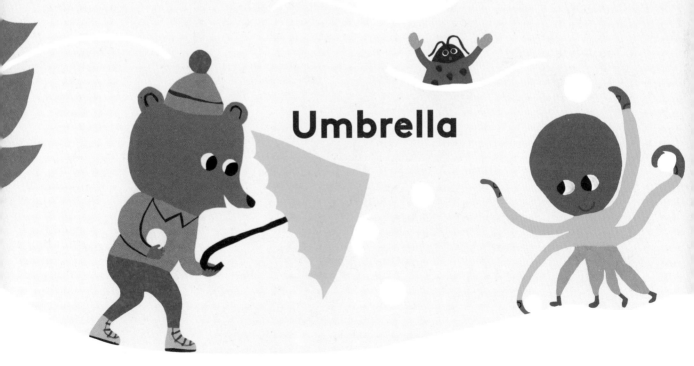

Brave

Worried

Surprised

Angry

Afraid

Happy

Sad

Hidden

Seen

Tall

Short

Small

Big

Loud

Hungry

I Can . . .

Stand

Listen

Sit

Walk

Talk

Laugh

Crawl

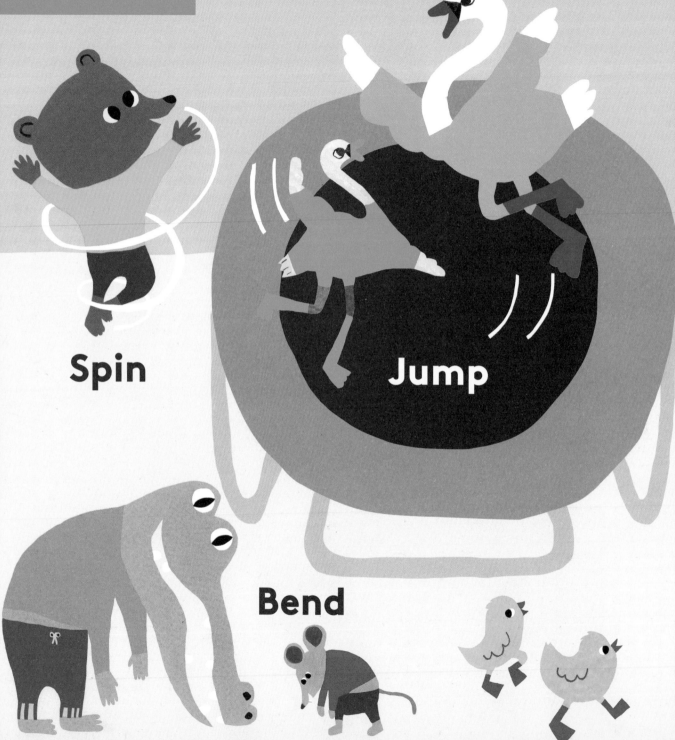

Spin

Jump

Bend

Stretch

Dance

Stamp

Roll

Awake

Drawer

Crib

Radio

Comb

3
2
1

Clock

Door

Toy

Living Room

Sofa

Cushion

Blind

Pot

Window

Goldfish

Tank

Bathroom

Shower

Soap

Bath

Faucet

Toothbrush

Sink

Toilet

Hallway

Lamp

Stairs

Telephone

Table

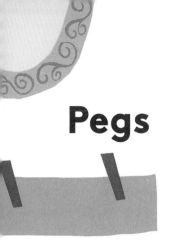

Pegs

Doorbell

10

Letters

Pot

Spoon

Bowl

Fork

Trash

Bib

Bite

Puzzle

Rattle

Blocks

Throw

Catch

Skip

Bounce

Bedtime

Moon

Night

Owl

Bear

Bottle

Sleep

Blanket

School

Morning

Wave

Gate

Classroom

Aa Bb Cc Dd Ee Ff
Gg Hh Ii Jj Kk Ll Mm
Nn Oo Pp Qq Rr Ss Tt
Uu Vv Ww Xx Yy Zz

Teacher

Learn

Pupil

Farm

Sheep

Barn

Chicken

Farmer

Chicks

Cloud

Cow

Goat

Pig

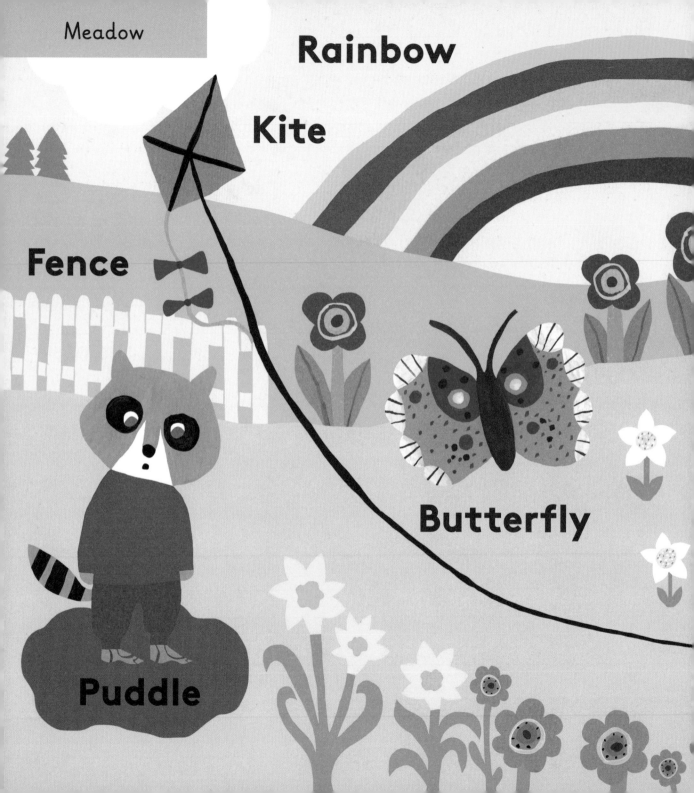

Meadow

Rainbow

Kite

Fence

Butterfly

Puddle

Deer

Hold

Sports Day

Team

Spring

Race

Running

Prize

Smile

Bumblebee

Nest

Frog

Bridge

Pond

Duck

Bird

Snail

Ceremony

Music

Wedding

Bride

Suit

Carriage

Drink

Eat

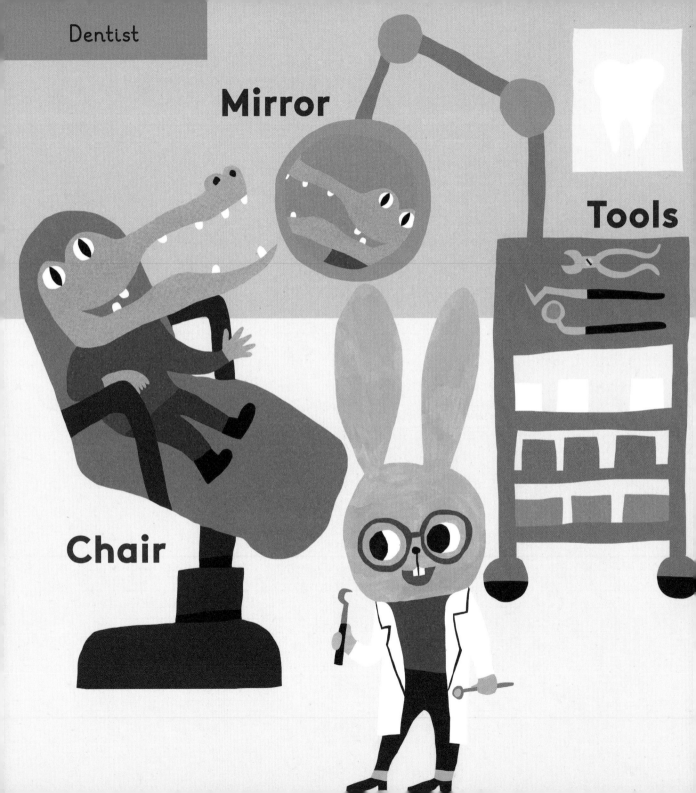

Dentist

Mirror

Tools

Chair

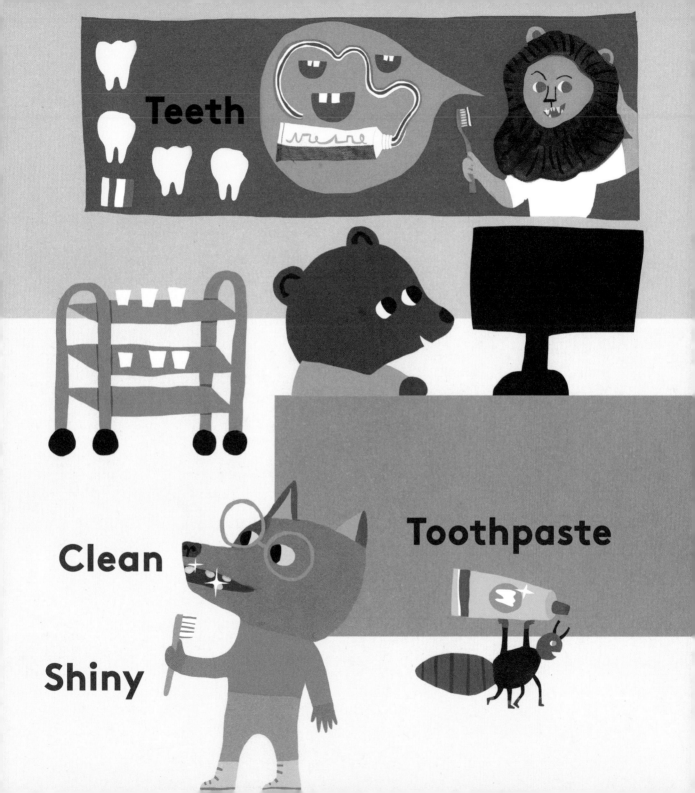

Teeth

Clean

Shiny

Toothpaste

Dive

Goggles

Splash

Towel

Pool

Float

Swim

Supermarket

Money

Purse

Groceries

Cart

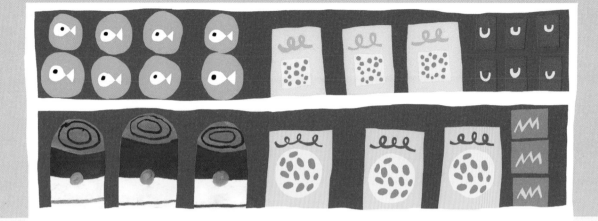

Food

Box

Job

Crab

Beach

Footprints

Shovel

Sand

Bucket

Shells

Zebra

Elephant

Lion

Alligator

Snake

Tiger

Giraffe

Travel

Airplane

Airport

Hotel

Arrive

Fly

Depart

Vacation

Picnic

Basket

Fruit

Bread

Cup

Plate

Mat

Stick

Courtside

Sun

Match

Tennis

Sky

Summer

Net

Shadow

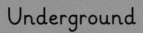

Fairy

Toadstool

Worm

Dig

Above

Tunnel

Below

Leaf

Trunk

Wind

Squirrel

Acorn

Tree

Autumn

Seesaw

Slide

Fountain

Bench

Playground

Climb

Stroller

Backyard

Game

Hose

Outside

Inside

Neighbor

Flower

Grass

Street

Rain

Bunch

Vegetable

Market

Stall

Sign

2 for 1

Bag

Castle

Crown

Queen

Pony

Treasure

King

Throne

Comfort

Doctor

Sick

Bed

Visitor

Greet

Painful

Medicine

Nurse

Library

Read

Speak

Quiet
please

Newspaper

Book

Shelf

Card

Magazine
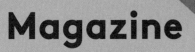

Theater

Light

Curtain

Chorus

Ribbon

Stage

Dancer

Clap

Artist

Picture

Pencil

Paint

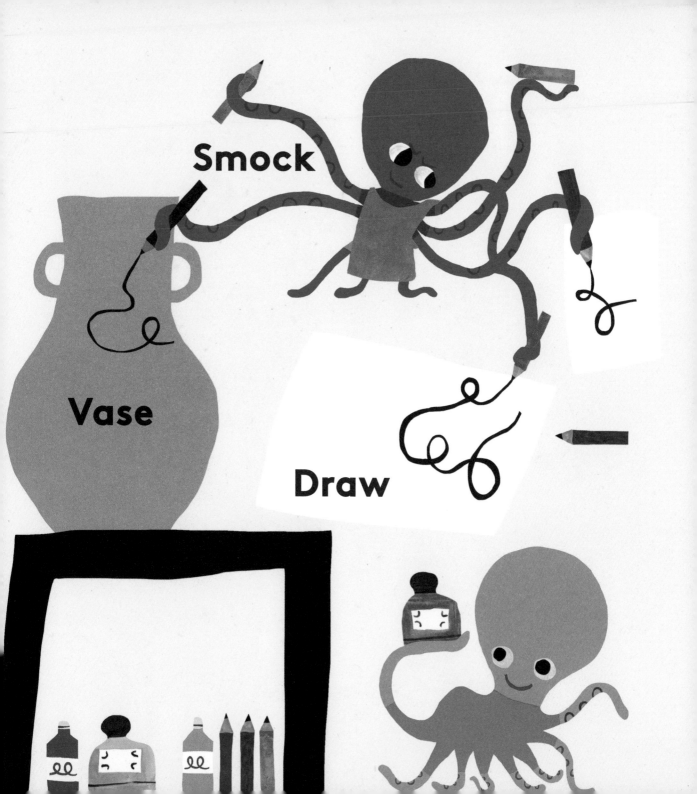

Smock

Vase

Draw

Party

Clown

Balloon

Gift

Funny

Flame

Candle

Cake

Ocean

Storm

Sailor

Ship

Whale

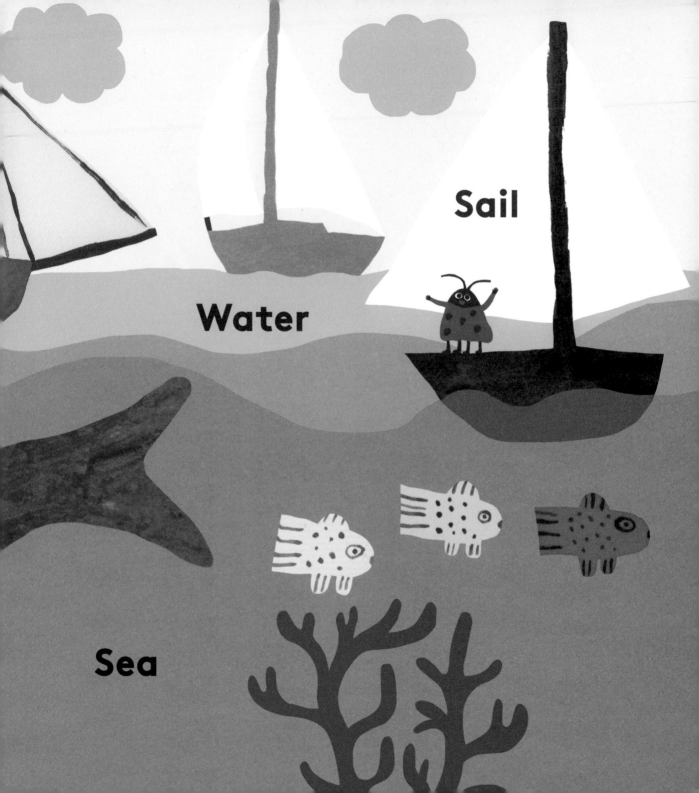

Sail

Water

Sea

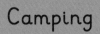

Tent

Hot

Fire

Map

Cabin

Flag

Cold

Truck

Ladder

Wood

Building

Hammer

Nail

Fix

Winter

Steep

Pull

Sled

Push

Hill

Ice

Soccer

Score

Kick

Handshake

Fog

Crowd

Goal

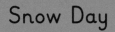

Snowflake

Gloves

Snow

Chocolate

Scarf

Skate

Hug

Boots

It's Never Too Early to Read with Your Child

Children love books, and they love spending one-on-one time sharing books with their caregivers.

One of the best ways to support your toddler and provide them with a solid foundation for learning is to build their understanding and knowledge of language. For decades, studies have shown the established link between a child's vocabulary size and academic success, and more recent studies have also shown a link to fewer anxiety-related issues, too.

By engaging in a simple reading activity every day, you are helping to give your child the best start in life.

Speak with your child

The quality of your interactions with your child is one of the biggest factors influencing their vocabulary. There are 365 words in this book, so use this book to introduce your child to the words, and then use those same words in conversations with your child as you go through your day. The more words your child hears and understands, the more they will be able to use.

Explore a world of words together

Young children have brains that soak up every experience, and they benefit from exposure to lots of words. Reading this book is an activity that the whole family can enjoy together. Use the same words in different kinds of sentences. See how often everyone in the family can use each word in everyday conversation.

Spark their imaginations

Talk about what interests your child, as it is more likely your child will pay attention and learn a new word. For example, if your child is interested in playing with cars, you can model words like "push" or "fast," or if they are interested in playing with a teddy bear, you can model words like "head" or "nose."

Say it again

Repeat words for your child on different occasions so it gives them more opportunities to hear and understand new words. Children's understanding of words precedes their use of words, and a child typically needs to hear a new word four to twelve times before it is added to their vocabulary.

Repeat and perfect

As your child attempts to pronounce new words, encourage them by repeating back what they've said, gently correcting any mispronounced sounds. For instance, if they point and say "Tat," reply with enthusiasm: "Yes, that is a cat, well done!"

Use pictures

Teach your child new words with pictures to help them visualize them. Each word in this book is positioned next to a correlating picture that will help teach your child the meaning of new words and to also pay attention and engage in a learning activity for short periods of time.

Explain what a new word means

Try to give new words context and explain their meaning using plain language to build your child's understanding of new words. For example, if you are looking at this book's page on vehicles and introduce the word "car," you could say something like "Can you see the car? Bear uses it to drive to places. It can go very fast! *Vrrm!*"

Actions can speak louder than words

Accompany your words with actions, gestures, or facial expressions to help your child understand the meaning of the words. For example, if you are modelling the word "sleep," you could point to the picture in the book of Bunny sleeping, or you could do a sleeping action (like hands under your head) so that your child understands what the word means.

Build on their success

As your child points to items in the book, label the items they do not yet know the names of. When your child correctly labels items themselves, encourage building their vocabulary further by acknowledging their successes and adding new words: "Yes! That is a bike. A shiny, red bike."

Let them grow at their own pace

Every child learns different things at a different pace, so try not to compare your child with anyone else's. Your little one will start talking when they are ready and, before you know it, they will be talking as a way of exploring the world in a whole new way.

The illustrations in this book were painted with gouache and composed digitally. Set in Brown and School Hand.

Library of Congress Control Number 2023937808

ISBN 978-1-4197-7131-6

Foreword by Meredith L. Rowe
Illustrations © 2022 Monika Forsberg
Text © 2022 Magic Cat Publishing
Cover © 2022 Magic Cat Publishing
Book design by Nicola Price

Printed and bound in China
10 9 8 7 6 5 4 3 2 1

Abrams Books are available at special discounts when purchased in quantity for premiums and promotions as well as fundraising or educational use. Special editions can also be created to specification. For details, contact specialsales@abramsbooks.com or the address below.

ABRAMS The Art of Books
195 Broadway, New York, NY 10007
abramsbooks.com